Wounds Of Life

Mrigendra Bharti

Published by Sellbrochure Vymish Entertainment, 2024.

WOUNDS OF LIFE

First edition. June 25, 2024.

ISBN: 979-8224530694

Written by Mrigendra Bharti.

Table of Contents

Preface

Life isn't always a bed of roses. We all experience wounds, big and small, that leave scars on our hearts and souls. "Wounds of Life" isn't meant to shy away from those scars. Instead, it delves into the raw emotions that accompany them – the sadness, the anger, the fear, and sometimes, the overwhelming sense of being lost.

But within these poems lies a flicker of hope. It's a testament to the human spirit's ability to weather storms, to find solace in unexpected places, and ultimately, to heal.

These poems are a collection of my own journeys through life's hardships, and the whispers of resilience I found along the way. Perhaps you'll see reflections of your own experiences within these verses. Perhaps you'll find comfort in knowing you're not alone.

This book is for anyone who has ever felt lost, anyone who carries the weight of the world on their shoulders, anyone searching for a flicker of hope in the darkness.

Welcome to the exploration of "Wounds of Life." May you find strength, solace, and a renewed sense of possibility within its pages.

Prologue

The world cracks open, not with a bang, but with the quiet sigh of a weathered hinge. Light spills through the fissure, revealing not a pristine landscape, but a tapestry woven with threads of gold and shadow. Here, laughter dances with tears, joy intertwines with sorrow, and hope flickers like a fragile candle in the wind.

This is the realm of scars, both physical and emotional, etched upon the canvas of life. Each mark tells a story – of battles fought and won, of burdens endured, of dreams chased and sometimes, tragically, lost. Yet, within the wounds lies a paradox. They are testaments to vulnerability, yes, but also to resilience. They are whispers of the past, yes, but also promises of the future.

We embark on a journey through these wounds, not to dwell on the pain, but to explore the lessons they hold. We will delve into the darkness, for it is there that we often find the most profound light. We will listen to the whispers of hope, for they are the embers that ignite the fire of the human spirit.

This is an invitation to confront your own wounds, to acknowledge their presence without succumbing to their weight. It is a call to embrace the vulnerability that makes you human, and to find strength in the very cracks that threaten to break you.

For within the wounds of life lies the potential for healing, for growth, and for a future etched not with pain, but with the unwavering courage of the human spirit. Are you ready to begin?

About Sellbrochure Vymish Entertainment

Sellbrochure Vymish Entertainment, recognized as India's largest book publishing company, has made significant strides in ensuring its extensive collection of books reaches audiences across the global market. This rapid expansion is a testament to the company's dedication to disseminating knowledge and literature far beyond national borders. Central to its success is its affiliation with InkWhirl Media Networks, a reputable entity in the media and publication industry known for its innovative and strategic approaches. Within this network, InkWhirl Publication LLC operates as a vital division, further enhancing the company's capabilities and reach in the international market. The visionary behind this enterprise is Mrigendra Bharti, the founder of Sellbrochure Vymish Entertainment. His foresight and passion for the literary world have been instrumental in steering the company towards remarkable growth and recognition. Under his leadership, Sellbrochure Vymish Entertainment has not only expanded its catalog but also established a strong presence in both domestic and international markets. Mrigendra Bharti's commitment to excellence and innovation has been a driving force in the company's journey, ensuring that it stays ahead of industry trends and meets the evolving needs of readers worldwide.

Sellbrochure Vymish Entertainment operates under the robust support of its parental organization, Mrigendra Bharti Group InfoTech. This affiliation provides the necessary resources and strategic guidance, enabling the publishing company to undertake ambitious projects and explore new markets. Mrigendra Bharti Group InfoTech's extensive experience in technology and information services has been a valuable asset, allowing Sellbrochure Vymish Entertainment to integrate advanced digital solutions in its operations, thereby enhancing its distribution capabilities and reader engagement.

Through relentless efforts and a commitment to quality, Sellbrochure Vymish Entertainment continues to break barriers and expand the reach of Indian literature globally. The company's diverse portfolio includes a wide range of genres, catering to different age groups and interests, thereby fostering a rich and inclusive reading culture. As it continues to innovate and grow, Sellbrochure Vymish Entertainment remains dedicated to its mission of making literature accessible to all, contributing significantly to the global literary landscape.

Connect With Mrigendra,
Thank you very much for choosing this book.
You can also connect with me on Instagram,
https://www.instagram.com/i_mrigendrabharti.official
With Love,
Mrigendra Bharti

Introduction

Life unfolds like a weathered map, its creases and folds marking the paths we've traveled. Some journeys are paved with golden sunlight, others shrouded in the storm's fury. Yet, etched upon this map are not just triumphant victories, but also the scars – the inevitable wounds we all encounter.

This collection, "Wounds of Life," isn't a morbid chronicle of pain. It delves into the raw vulnerability that accompanies these wounds – the sting of loss, the weight of burdens, the hollowness of despair. We'll explore these emotions with unflinching honesty, for within them lies a potent truth about the human experience.

But "Wounds of Life" isn't solely a descent into darkness. It's a testament to the resilience that flickers within each of us. You'll find whispers of hope tucked within the verses – whispers that remind us of our inherent strength, the unexpected pockets of beauty that emerge even from hardship, and the unwavering spirit that propels us forward.

Prepare to encounter poems that act as mirrors, reflecting experiences you may recognize – the ache of a broken heart, the burden of unfulfilled dreams, the quiet strength that emerges in the face of adversity. Perhaps you'll find solace in this shared vulnerability, a sense of belonging in the knowledge that you're not alone on this journey.

These poems are more than just words on a page; they are invitations. Invitations to confront your own wounds, to acknowledge their presence without succumbing to their weight. They are invitations to embrace the very cracks that threaten to break you, for within them lies the potential for profound healing and growth.

So, turn the page, dear reader, and embark on this exploration of the human experience. Let's delve into the wounds of life, not to dwell on the pain, but to discover the strength, resilience, and the unwavering hope that resides within them.

A Ray of Hope

Don't give up, don't lose hope,
Life has just begun,
There are many paths left, many destinations left,
It's not time to give up yet.
So what if you lose some, learn from your losses,
Correct your mistakes, move forward,
You gain something from every try,
This is the journey of life.
Let the ray of hope burn,
Don't let the fire of courage go out,
Keep walking on the hard paths,
One day you will surely succeed.

Incomplete Journey

Steps faltered, defeat accepted,
Dreams' castle collapsed,
Incomplete journey, unfinished story,
Only a sea of pain in the eyes left.
The bird had a desire to fly,
But the support of the wings broke,
Fell helpless on the ground,
Lost the sight of the sky.
I thought I would make a name,
I will make my mark in the world,
But gave up nameless,
Leaving behind an incomplete journey, an unfinished story.
What will happen next? I don't know,
There is only emptiness in my heart,
Incomplete journey, unfinished story,
That's all that will remain in life.

This Is Not the Time to Stop

There will be stumbles and recoveries,
Every path will have a turn,
But don't get tired, traveler, keep moving,
This is not the time to stop.
The wind keeps changing direction,
So what if there's failure today,
The sun will shine again tomorrow,
This is not the time to stop.
There's a new lesson in every attempt,
Every failure is a stepping stone,
The destination is far, but stay hopeful,
This is not the time to stop.

The Seed of Resilience

Though storms may bend and break the bough,
The roots endure, unseen below.
Though efforts fail, and dreams lie low,
A seed of strength begins to grow.
Within the heart, where shadows play,
A quiet strength will find its way.
For in the pause, the lessons stay,
To guide us on a brighter day.
The path we walk may twist and turn,
But lessons learned, at fires we've burned,
Will help us rise, with spirit yearned,
For even failures, wisely earned.

In the Depths of Despair

In the depths of despair, I find myself lost,
Adrift in a sea of sorrows, at a tremendous cost.
My dreams have shattered, my hopes have died,
And the weight of defeat, I cannot hide.
I've fought with all my might, with every ounce of my soul,
But the winds of adversity, have taken their toll.
My spirit is broken, my heart filled with pain,
As I face the reality, that I've lost the game.
The path I once envisioned, now fades into gray,
The future I once cherished, has slipped away.
The laughter and joy, have turned into tears,
As I drown in the depths, of my darkest fears.
I yearn for a glimmer, of light in the gloom,
But the shadows surround me, consuming the room.
No beacon of hope, no guiding star,
Just the echoes of failure, from afar.
I'm lost in the labyrinth, of my own despair,
With no way out, no breath of fresh air.
The weight of the world, is crushing my chest,
As I succumb to the darkness, and take my last rest.

Ashes to Hope

The flames of ambition, once burned so bright,
Now smolder and flicker, a fading light.
Defeat's bitter ashes, cling to my face,
A testament to failure, a lonely embrace.
The weight of the world, a crushing despair,
Drags me downwards, burdens to bear.
But embers still whisper, a voice from within,
A fire unconquered, a battle to win.
From the ruins of failure, a strength will arise,
A spirit reborn, with a new set of eyes.
The path may be hidden, the future unclear,
But hope's tiny ember will conquer my fear.
I'll rise from the ashes, and walk through the night,
With the flames of resilience, burning ever so bright.

The Unbroken Seed

Beneath the rubble of shattered dreams,
Where shadows whisper of what might have been,
A tiny seed of hope remains unseen.
Bruised and battered, it struggles to breathe,
Lost in the darkness, where doubt takes its leave.
But the will to survive, a fierce undercurrent,
Pushes against despair, a silent current.
For even in darkness, a seed holds the light,
A promise of springtime, a future so bright.
Though the path ahead may be shrouded in gray,
The unbroken seed whispers, "There's a new dawn someday."

The Broken Wing

My wings, once mighty, now lie tattered and torn,
Dreams dashed upon the rocks, where hope is forlorn.
The wind of misfortune, a cruel, bitter blow,
Has sent me plummeting down, to the depths below.
In this inky darkness, where shadows reside,
No solace remains, no place to confide.
The weight of defeat, a crushing despair,
Steals the breath from my lungs, fills my heart with a tear.
But embers still flicker, a faint, dying light,
A whisper that urges, to take flight once more.
Though the journey seems endless, the path veiled in gray,
A sliver of hope fights for dawn's early ray.
For even the broken, can rise from the fall,
Spread tattered wings wide, and answer the call.
This fight may be weary, the scars etched in deep,
But the spirit unbroken, will rise from its sleep.

Whispers in the Storm

The storm rages on, a relentless assault,
Raining down failures, on dreams I once sought.
Lightning of doubt splits the darkening sky,
Thunder of anguish, a deafening cry.
Lost in the tempest, I stumble and fall,
Hope's fragile ember, flickering so small.
The weight of the world, a suffocating hold,
Buries me deeper, in stories untold.
But wait, in the distance, a whisper I hear,
A voice soft and gentle, dispelling my fear.
It speaks of resilience, of strength yet unseen,
A fire within, waiting to be keen.
The storm may not cease, but I rise from the mud,
Washed clean by the tears, misunderstood.
Hope rekindled, a flame burning bright,
I'll weather the storm, and find my own light.

Embers of Resilience

The path I once walked, now shrouded in mist,
Dreams turned to ashes, a future unkissed.
The weight of the world, a burden so vast,
Crushing my spirit, a tempest that blasts.
Stars that once shone, have dimmed and grown cold,
Their guiding light lost, a story untold.
Despair's icy grip, threatens to freeze,
Leaving me numb, on my desperate knees.
But wait, a faint ember, a flicker of gold,
Flickers within me, a story untold.
A whisper of strength, a will to hold fast,
A flicker of hope, that this darkness won't last.
Though the journey ahead may be shrouded in night,
This ember of resilience will burn ever so bright.
I'll rise from the ashes, and face the unknown,
For even in darkness, a new seed is sown.

Lost in the Labyrinth

I wander through pathways, shrouded in fog,
My memories tainted, a mournful monologue.
Hope's compass is broken, the map fades from sight,
Lost in a labyrinth, where shadows take flight.
The weight of defeat, a burden I hold,
A story of failures, whispered and told.
Stars once so brilliant, now distant and dim,
A yearning for solace, a haunting hymn.
But wait, in the silence, a whisper so frail,
A voice that reminds me, I haven't yet failed.
A flicker of embers, a promise unseen,
A strength yet untapped, a spirit serene.
Though lost in the darkness, I'll search for the dawn,
With courage as my compass, I'll carry on.
For even in darkness, a seed can take root,
And bloom in defiance, bearing hope's sweet fruit.

The Ashen Heart

My heart, once a furnace, where dreams burned so bright,
Now lies dormant and ashen, devoid of its light.
The fuel of ambition, extinguished by strife,
Leaving behind hollow echoes of a passionate life.
The weight of the world, a relentless cascade,
Crushes my spirit, leaving hope to erode.
Shadows lengthen and twist, mocking aspirations,
Taunting me with memories of grand creations.
But wait, a faint ember, a spark in the gloom,
A flicker of defiance, refusing to succumb.
A whisper arises, a voice from within,
Reminding me gently, a new path can begin.
For even the ashes, hold the promise of fire,
A chance to rekindle, and rise ever higher.
Though the journey is daunting, the scars etched so deep,
The ashen heart remembers, the embers to keep.

Drowning in Doubt

The weight of the world, a crushing embrace,
Drags me downwards, a tear-stained face.
Doubt's icy fingers, grip my fragile soul,
Pulling me deeper, where shadows take hold.
The whispers of triumph, now distant and frail,
Replaced by echoes of failure's sad tale.
Hope's buoyant lantern, sputters and fades,
Lost in the darkness, a future that evades.
But wait, a faint tremor, a spark in the gloom,
A flicker of defiance, refusing to tomb.
A voice, soft and gentle, whispers within,
"Though the path is obscured, there's strength to begin."

Ashes to Hope

The flames of ambition, once burned so bright,
Now smolder and flicker, a fading light.
Defeat's bitter ashes, cling to my face,
A testament to failure, a lonely embrace.
The weight of the world, a crushing despair,
Drags me downwards, burdens to bear.
But embers still whisper, a voice from within,
A fire unconquered, a battle to win.
From the ruins of failure, a strength will arise,
A spirit reborn, with a new set of eyes.
The path may be hidden, the future unclear,
But hope's tiny ember will conquer my fear.

The Broken Wing

My wings, once mighty, now lie tattered and torn,

Dreams dashed upon rocks, where hope is forlorn.

The wind of misfortune, a cruel, bitter blow,

Has sent me plummeting down, to the depths below.

In this inky darkness, where shadows reside,

No solace remains, no place to confide.

The weight of defeat, a crushing despair,

Steals the breath from my lungs, fills my heart with a tear.

But embers still flicker, a faint, dying light,

A whisper that urges, to take flight once more.

Though the journey seems endless, the path veiled in gray,

A sliver of hope fights for dawn's early ray.

The Invincible Seed

Though storms may rage on, and skies turn to lead,
A tiny seed slumbers, a hope yet unfed.
Beneath layers of doubt, and burdens untold,
A strength perseveres, braver than cold.
The whispers of failure, a deafening din,
May try to extinguish the fire within.
But life seeks a chance, with an unwavering hold,
The invincible seed, yearning to unfold.
For even in darkness, where shadows reside,
The seed of resilience, cannot be denied.
It waits for the sunlight, to break through the night,
And bloom with defiance, a beacon of light.

Aching Silence

The world spins around me, a symphony loud,
But all I perceive is a deafening shroud.
The cheers and the laughter, fall silent and dim,
Lost in the echo of my battles within.
The weight of the world, a burden immense,
Steals the rhythm from life, its joyful pretense.
Hope's melody fades, a whisper unheard,
Leaving behind silence, a lonely, gray word.
But wait, in the hush, a faint beating drum,
A steady resilience, refusing to succumb.
The silence transforms, a canvas so bare,
A chance to rewrite, a future to share.

Fractured

The mirror I held, reflecting my soul,
Now fractured and splintered, losing control.
Each shard unveils a piece of the fight,
A mosaic of struggles, bathed in dim light.
The weight of the world, a relentless tide,
Threatens to drown me, where dreams used to reside.
Hope's fragile tendrils, frayed and worn thin,
Yearn for the sun, a chance to begin.
But see, in the cracks, a glimmer remains,
A chance to mend, to rise from the pains.
For even the broken can be made whole,
Picking up pieces to reclaim their goal.

Embers of Defiance

The path I once walked, now veiled in despair,
Dreams turned to ashes, a future to bear.
The weight of the world, a burden untold,
Crushing my spirit, a story grown cold.
The stars that once guided, now distant and dim,
A flicker of doubt, a haunting hymn.
Despair's icy grip, tightening its hold,
Leaving me numb, a future unsold.
But wait, a faint ember, a spark in the night,
A flicker of defiance, a burning so bright.
A whisper of strength, a will to ignite,
Hope's embers rekindled, refusing to die.
Though the journey may darken, with twists and with turns,
These embers of defiance, a fire that burns.
I'll rise from the ashes, and step into the unknown,
For even in darkness, a new seed is sown.

The Weight of the World

The weight of the world, a crushing embrace,
Squeezes the laughter, from my weary face.
Doubt's heavy cloak, a suffocating hold,
Drags me down deeper, a story untold.
The whispers of triumph, a distant refrain,
Replaced by the echoes of sorrow and pain.
Hope's fragile vessel, tossed on the waves,
Lost in the tempest, where no sunlight saves.
But wait, in the depths, a flicker ignites,
A spark of defiance, that burns ever so bright.
A voice from within, whispers soft and clear,
"Though the path is obscured, there's strength to persevere."

Aching Beauty

The world throbs with color, a vibrant display,
But all I perceive is a canvas of gray.
The laughter and sunshine, fall muted and dim,
Lost in the shadows, where hope used to swim.
The weight of the world, a burden so deep,
Steals the vibrancy, where dreams used to sleep.
Hope's melody fades, a whisper unheard,
Leaving behind silence, a lonely gray word.
But wait, in the hush, a beauty remains,
A world yet unseen, untouched by the pains.
For even in darkness, the senses ignite,
Aching for beauty, a reason to fight.
These poems explore the depths of despair, but also offer a
glimmer of hope and the enduring strength to rise above it.

Hollow Victory

The battle is won, the spoils at my feet,
But victory feels hollow, bittersweet.
The cost of the triumph, a heavy toll paid,
A landscape of losses, in victory's parade.
The weight of the world, a burden of scars,
Memories whisper of fallen comrades, of wars.
Hope wears a mask, a smile that's strained,
A victory dance, in emotions restrained.
Yet, embers still flicker, a promise unseen,
To rebuild from ashes, a future serene.
For even in triumph, a lesson remains,
The true price of victory, etched in the veins.

Whispers in the Canyon

The canyon walls echo, with silence untold,
A vast, empty canvas, where dreams turn cold.
The wind whispers secrets, of failures long past,
Each gust a reminder, of battles surpassed.
The weight of the world, a crushing despair,
Settles in the canyons, a heavy, cold air.
Hope's fragile compass, spins lost and unsure,
No guiding direction, on this barren moor.
But wait, in the distance, a flicker appears,
A lone desert flower, defying the years.
A whisper of resilience, on the wind's gentle sigh,
A reminder that life finds a way, even when dreams die.

The Weathered Soul

Wrinkles etched deep, a map of life's strife,
Each line a reminder, of battles for life.
The eyes, once so bright, now hold a soft gleam,
A weathered soul's wisdom, in a fading dream.
The weight of the world, a burden well known,
Carried with grace, on a journey alone.
Hope's embers still flicker, though faint and subdued,
A quiet acceptance, of battles pursued.
Yet, the weathered soul whispers, a story untold,
Of resilience triumphant, braver than bold.
For even in twilight, wisdom remains,
A legacy etched, in the heart's gentle strains.

Masquerade of Joy

Laughter rings hollow, a mask I portray,
Hiding the darkness, that eats me away.
A performance of joy, for the world to behold,
While my spirit crumbles, a story untold.
The weight of the world, a burden unseen,
A silent struggle, on a stage so keen.
Hope's fragile facade, threatens to crack,
A masquerade crumbling, with a deafening lack.
But wait, in the depths, a strength takes its stand,
A voice whispers courage, with a firm, steady hand.
The mask may be shattered, the truth may appear,
But vulnerability holds strength, casting out fear.

The Unwritten Symphony

The score lies abandoned, a melody lost,
A symphony unplayed, at a terrible cost.
The instruments silent, their voices unheard,
A canvas of silence, where feelings are stirred.
The weight of the world, a crushing despair,
Stifles the music, leaving only the air.
Hope's fragile strings, lie broken and frayed,
A symphony silenced, a future dismayed.
But wait, a faint tremor, a whisper within,
A fragment of music, a yearning to begin.
The composer awakens, with a fire anew,
To rewrite the symphony, with a heart strong and true.

Shattered Glass and Shattered Dreams

The mirror I held, a portal of pride,
Now lies in a million pieces, dreams cast aside.
Each shard a reflection, a memory's sting,
Of futures envisioned, on broken hope's wing.
The weight of the world, a crushing embrace,
Squeezes the laughter from my weary face.
Doubt's icy fingers, grip tight and constrict,
Leaving me lost in the shadows, adrift.
But wait, in the silence, a flicker so faint,
A whisper of strength, a defiant complaint.
For even the broken, can gather the light,
And piece by piece, rebuild a future so bright.

Whispers in the Static

The radio crackles, a symphony frayed,
Distorted messages, of hope that's decayed.
Static devours voices, once comforting and true,
Leaving a void where solace used to accrue.
The weight of the world, a burden so vast,
Steals the connection, a future surpassed.
Hope's fragile signal, lost in the noise,
A desperate yearning for guiding, clear voice.
But wait, in the fuzz, a frequency breaks through,
A message of resilience, urging me to pursue.
For even in static, a connection remains,
A spark of resistance, defying the strains.

The Unspoken Tear

Tears well in my eyes, a silent cascade,
But social convention, demands a charade.
A stiff upper lip, a smile plastered on,
The weight of emotions, forever withdrawn.
The weight of the world, a burden untold,
Fears and frustrations, silently unfold.
Hope's fragile mask, strained and unsure,
Yearning for release, a moment to pour.
But wait, in the silence, a strength finds its voice,
The unspoken tear, a powerful choice.
For even in silence, emotions can rise,
A cleansing cascade, cleansing clouded skies.

The Faded Canvas

The painting I cherished, vibrant and bold,
Now hangs faded and weary, a story untold.
Colors once bright, now muted and dim,
A reflection of struggles, a fading hymn.
The weight of the world, a relentless tide,
Erases the beauty, where dreams used to reside.
Hope's fragile brushstrokes, worn and unclear,
Leaving the canvas empty, a future austere.
But wait, in the corner, a flicker of hue,
A spark of inspiration, a promise brand new.
The artist awakens, with a vision renewed,
To paint a new canvas, vibrant and subdued.

The Weightless Cage

Invisible bars, a cage I can't see,
Confines my spirit, relentlessly.
Fear holds the key, a warden so keen,
Trapping my potential, a life yet unseen.
The weight of the world, a burden of thought,
A self-made prison, a battle unfought.
Hope's fragile wings, clipped and confined,
Yearning for freedom, a peace of mind.
But wait, in the silence, a voice whispers low,
A reminder of strength, that helps the spirit grow.
The cage can be broken, with courage as guide,
To soar through the sky, with hope at my side.

The Borrowed Smile

The world smiles around me, a symphony bright,
But the smile I wear, is borrowed, not mine.
A mask of contentment, hiding the strife,
A silent performance, on the stage of life.
The weight of the world, a burden unseen,
Aching within, where laughter should have been.
Hope's fragile thread, a whisper unheard,
Lost in the chorus of merriment's word.
But wait, in the depths, a flicker remains,
A yearning for truth, to wash away stains.
The borrowed smile fades, a curtain withdrawn,
To face vulnerability, a strength yet unborn.

Whispers in the Fog

The path stretches forward, shrouded in mist,
A future uncertain, a future unkissed.
Footsteps uncertain, lost in the white,
Hope's guiding compass, lost in the night.
The weight of the world, a burden so vast,
Blurs the horizon, a desolate fast.
Doubt's icy fingers, grip tight and constrict,
Leaving me stranded, lost in self-inflicted plight.
But wait, a faint tremor, a whisper within,
A voice urging courage, to break through the skin.
For even in fog, a path can be made,
One step at a time, out of the shade.

The Hollow Echo

Laughter rings out, in the crowded room,
But my own laughter, echoes in a tomb.
The joy vibrates fiercely, a foreign display,
A hollow echo, where my spirit can't stray.
The weight of the world, a burden of stone,
Drags me down deeper, emotions unknown.
Hope's fragile flame, flickers and wanes,
A yearning for connection, that soothes the body's pains.
But wait, in the silence, a warmth takes its hold,
A hand reaches out, a story untold.
The hollow echo fades, replaced by a touch,
A reminder of kindness, compassion's clutch.

The Faded Photograph

The photograph whispers, of a time long ago,
A vibrant reflection, with a joyful glow.
Eyes filled with dreams, smiles wide and bright,
A forgotten melody, lost in the night.
The weight of the world, a burden of time,
Has dimmed the laughter, replaced with a rhyme.
Hope's fragile portrait, faded and worn,
A haunting reminder, of a future unborn.
But wait, in the creases, a message survives,
A whisper of strength, where resilience thrives.
For even in fading, the spirit remains,
Embracing the journey, and the wisdom it gains.

The Whispering Wind

The wind whispers secrets, through trees tall and strong,
A symphony woven, where hope sings along.
Leaves dance and rustle, a language unknown,
Yet a comfort it offers, in a world on its own.
The weight of the world, a burden that bends,
Threatens to break me, where solace suspends.
Hope's fragile thread, pulled taut and so thin,
Yearning for an anchor, to pull me back in.
But wait, in the rustling, a message takes flight,
A whisper of resilience, a beacon so bright.
The wind carries stories, of struggles overcome,
A reminder that nature, finds a way to become.

The Weeping Willow

The willow weeps softly, its branches cascade,
Mirroring the tears, that my spirit has made.
Leaves droop and descend, in a sorrowful sigh,
A reflection of burdens, beneath a tearful sky.
The weight of the world, a crushing embrace,
Stifles the laughter, from this lonely space.
Hope's fragile bud, withers and shrinks,
Lost in the shadows, where despair inks.
But wait, in the weeping, a strength takes its root,
A silent resilience, bearing sorrow's mute fruit.
For even in tears, life finds a way,
To nourish and blossom, come another bright day.

Whispers in the Fire

The flames lick and dance, a mesmerizing sight,
But the warmth they offer, fails to ignite.
Smoke billows upwards, carrying dreams unfurled,
Leaving behind ashes, in a broken world.
The weight of the world, a smothering hold,
Steals the fire's passion, leaving stories untold.
Hope's embers lie dormant, a flicker unseen,
Lost in the darkness, where shadows convene.
But wait, in the embers, a spark faintly glows,
A whisper of defiance, against life's harsh blows.
For even in darkness, fire can ignite,
Transforming the ashes, with a renewed light.

The Starless Night

The velvet expanse, devoid of starlight,
A canvas of darkness, on this lonely night.
No guiding beacons, to pierce the black veil,
Leaving me stranded, lost in a hopeless tale.
The weight of the world, a burden so vast,
Crushes my spirit, holding the future fast.
Hope's fragile compass, spins lost and unsure,
No direction to follow, no path to endure.
But wait, in the distance, a faint, silver gleam,
A solitary star, defying the dream.
A whisper of strength, in the inky expanse,
A reminder that even in darkness, faith can take a chance.

The Broken Compass

The compass I cherished, a guide on life's way,
Now lies shattered and splintered, with nothing to say.
The needle spins wildly, lost and unsure,
No direction to follow, no future to secure.
The weight of the world, a burden of doubt,
Leaves me adrift, with no map to find out.
Hope's fragile path, obscured and unseen,
Lost in a labyrinth, where shadows convene.
But wait, in the stillness, a voice whispers low,
A compass within, a strength yet to grow.
The broken may mend, with courage as guide,
For even lost paths, can lead to places untried.

Whispers in the Rain

The rain falls in torrents, a relentless cascade,
Washing away dreams, leaving emotions unsaid.
The world weeps with me, in a symphony gray,
Mirroring the sorrow, that clouds my own day.
The weight of the world, a burden of tears,
Steals the sunshine's warmth, from my forgotten years.
Hope's fragile wings, drenched and unable to fly,
Lost in the downpour, with a sorrowful cry.
But wait, in the pitter-patter, a message takes hold,
A cleansing rhythm, a story untold.
The rain washes clean, a chance to begin,
Renewed and refreshed, to let hope back in.

The Songbird's Silence

The songbird sits silent, its melody stilled,
No joyful tunes echo, on the wind's gentle trill.
A weight on its feathers, a burden unseen,
The music imprisoned, in a world harsh and mean.
The weight of the world, a crushing despair,
Stifles the laughter, leaving only the air.
Hope's forgotten song, lost in the night,
A yearning for freedom, to take flight.
But wait, in the stillness, a tremor takes hold,
A whisper of courage, a story untold.
The songbird remembers, a melody deep,
And gathers its strength, from slumber's soft sleep.

Whispers in the Moonlight

The moon casts a pale glow, on a world cold and stark,
A canvas of shadows, where dreams leave their mark.
Stars dim and distant, offer no guiding light,
Leaving me stranded, in the lonely night.
The weight of the world, a burden immense,
Steals the warmth from life, leaving a chilling suspense.
Hope's fragile flame, flickers and wanes,
A desperate yearning, to escape the body's pains.
But wait, in the moonlight, a glimmer appears,
A whisper of solace, dispelling the fears.
For even in darkness, the moon holds its sway,
Guiding the lost, with its gentle, ethereal ray.

The Cracked Mirror

The mirror reflects, a distorted portrayal,
A fractured image, of a life gone astray.
Each shard a reminder, of battles unwon,
A broken reflection, beneath a setting sun.
The weight of the world, a burden of scars,
Etched on the surface, like fallen stars.
Hope's fragile mask, shattered and cracked,
Leaving the spirit weary, a future attacked.
But wait, in the pieces, a strength can reside,
A chance to reassemble, with a newfound pride.
For even the broken, can reflect a new light,
Emerging from fragments, with a future more bright.

The Fading Flower

The vibrant bloom withers, once proud and so bold,
Petals droop and surrender, a story untold.
Colors once dazzling, now dulled and subdued,
A metaphor for dreams, misunderstood.
The weight of the world, a burden so vast,
Drains the life essence, holding the future fast.
Hope's fragile thread, withers and fades,
Lost in the silence, where beauty pervades.
But wait, in the fading, a promise remains,
A whisper of resilience, defying the strains.
For even the wilted, hold seeds within,
Waiting for sunshine, a new life to begin.

Whispers in the Desert

The sand stretches endless, a vast, barren plain,
A desolate landscape, devoid of life's rain.
Sun beats down fiercely, on a world cracked and dry,
A reflection of struggle, with a tearful cry.
The weight of the world, a crushing despair,
Stifles the laughter, leaving only the air.
Hope's fragile oasis, a distant mirage,
Lost in a wasteland, consumed by its rage.
But wait, in the silence, a whisper takes flight,
A resilient spirit, bathed in the desert's light.
For even in dryness, life finds a hold,
Adapting and thriving, a story untold.

The Borrowed Mask

A painted smile I wear, a borrowed facade,
Hiding the storm within, emotions unswayed.
Laughter rings hollow, a performance in vain,
Masking the heartache, the burdens that strain.
The weight of the world, a cloak I can't shed,
Drags me down deeper, where dreams lie half-dead.
Hope's fragile flame flickers, a candle unseen,
Yearning for truth, to break free, serene.
But wait, in the silence, a voice whispers low,
A strength to be honest, to let feelings flow.
The borrowed mask crumbles, revealing the core,
A chance to be vulnerable, and hope to explore.

Whispers in the Crowds

The city's a symphony, a cacophony bright,
Strangers and faces, a rushing, fast light.
Lost in the throng, a voice unheard, unseen,
An island of sadness, in a world so keen.
The weight of the world, a burden of doubt,
Shrouds me in loneliness, a silent shout.
Hope's fragile thread, tangled in the noise,
A yearning for connection, a voice that enjoys.
But wait, in the bustle, a hand reaches out,
A smile from a stranger, dispelling the drought.
The crowds become faces, with stories untold,
A chance for connection, worth more than gold.

The Unspoken Name

The name hangs unspoken, a memory held tight,
A ghost from the past, in the dead of the night.
A whisper of laughter, a touch and a tear,
A love that is lost, a wound ever near.
The weight of the world, a burden of grief,
Stifles the laughter, brings no sweet relief.
Hope's fragile thread, stained with the pain,
Struggling to mend, a future to gain.
But wait, in the silence, a whisper takes flight,
A voice of acceptance, bathed in soft light.
The name can be spoken, with love and with grace,
Releasing the sorrow, and finding a space.

The Faded Photograph (a different take)

The photograph whispers, of dreams long gone by,
A bittersweet memory, with a tear in my eye.
Eyes filled with wonder, a future unplanned,
Lessons still echo, a hand in my hand.
The weight of the world, a burden of time,
Has etched on my features, a wisdom sublime.
Hope's fragile portrait, though faded and worn,
Holds a reminder, of where I was born.
But wait, in the creases, a message survives,
A whisper of courage, where experience thrives.
For even in fading, the spirit's alive,
Embracing the journey, and the strength it can give.

Whispers in the Storm (a different take)

The tempest roars fiercely, a symphony strong,
Rain lashes like tears, as the world rights a wrong.
Lightning illuminates, a cleansing display,
Washing away doubts, on this tempestuous day.
The weight of the world, a burden released,
Emotions unleashed, a storm long appeased.
Hope's fragile vessel, tossed on the waves,
Rides the storm's fury, embracing the braves.
But wait, in the thunder, a message rings true,
A voice of resilience, born anew.
For even in darkness, the storm has its grace,
A chance for renewal, to find a new space.

The Weeping Sky

The heavens weep openly, a curtain of gray,
Mirroring the tears, that fall night and day.
Each drop a reflection, of burdens untold,
A symphony of sadness, on a world turned cold.
The weight of the world, a crushing embrace,
Squeezes the laughter, from this lonely space.
Hope's fragile umbrella, tattered and torn,
Leaving the spirit drenched, on a future forlorn.
But wait, in the downpour, a whisper takes hold,
A cleansing rhythm, a story untold.
The weeping sky mourns, for burdens released,
A chance for renewal, a spirit appeased.

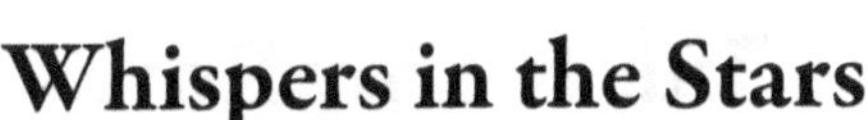

Whispers in the Stars

The vast expanse twinkles, a tapestry bright,
A million tiny whispers, guiding through the night.
Constellations beckon, with stories untold,
Of journeys and struggles, braver than bold.
The weight of the world, a burden immense,
Steals the wonder from life, leaving a chilling suspense.
Hope's fragile compass, lost and unsure,
No direction to follow, no future to secure.
But wait, in the twinkling, a message appears,
A whisper of guidance, dispelling the fears.
For even in darkness, the stars brightly shine,
Guiding lost travelers, with a light so divine.

The Thorny Rose

The rose blooms defiant, with thorns sharp and strong,
A beauty protected, from the world's careless throng.
Fragile petals unfurl, a vibrant display,
A symbol of strength, hidden in a graceful way.
The weight of the world, a burden so vast,
Threatens to crush the beauty, beauty built to last.
Hope's fragile bloom, withers under the strain,
Yearning for sunlight, to blossom again.
But wait, in the thorns, a message resides,
A whisper of resilience, where beauty confides.
For even the vulnerable, can rise from the fight,
Emerging triumphant, with thorns shining bright.

The Fading Flame

The fire crackles softly, embers dim and low,
A fading warmth lingers, where passion used to flow.
Smoke curls and dances, a memory's refrain,
A reminder of dreams, lost in the pouring rain.
The weight of the world, a smothering hold,
Steals the fire's passion, leaving stories untold.
Hope's fragile flame flickers, a dying ember's glow,
Lost in the shadows, where dreams ebb and flow.
But wait, in the embers, a spark faintly gleams,
A whisper of resilience, against life's harsh streams.
For even in darkness, a flame can ignite,
Transforming the ashes, with a renewed light.

Whispers in the Leaves

The wind whispers secrets, through leaves light and green,
A symphony rustling, a vibrant, unseen.
Branches sway gently, a language so free,
A message of hope, for all who can see.
The weight of the world, a burden that bends,
Threatens to break me, where solace suspends.
Hope's fragile thread, pulled taut and so thin,
Yearning for an anchor, to pull me back in.
But wait, in the rustling, a message takes flight,
A whisper of nature, bathed in soft light.
The leaves dance and whisper, of cycles untold,
Of endings and beginnings, braver than bold.

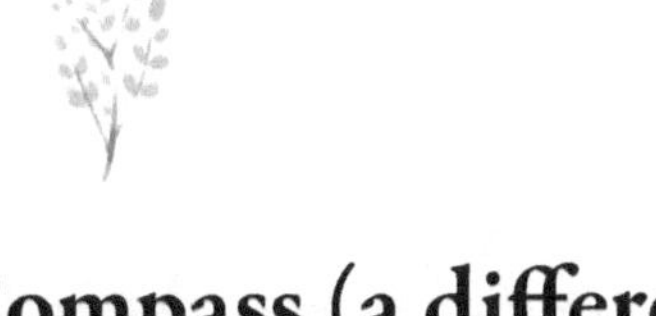

The Broken Compass (a different take)

The compass lies shattered, its needle askew,
No north to be found, no direction holds true.
Lost in the wilderness, with choices unclear,
A journey uncertain, filled with doubt and with fear.
The weight of the world, a burden of choice,
Leads down winding paths, with a muffled voice.
Hope's fragile map, crumpled and torn,
Leaving the wanderer stranded, a future unborn.
But wait, in the wreckage, a whisper ignites,
A strength from within, guiding through the nights.
For even lost paths, hold beauty unseen,
A chance for adventure, where courage has been.

Whispers in the Fog (a different take)

The fog obscures vision, a world turned opaque,
A path disappears, with no future to take.
Footsteps uncertain, on a journey unplanned,
Lost in the silence, with questions unmanned.
The weight of the world, a burden unknown,
Hides destinations, leaving me all alone.
Hope's fragile lantern, dimmed by the mist,
Yearning for clarity, where purpose insists.
But wait, in the stillness, a voice whispers low,
A message of courage, helping the spirit to grow.
For even in fog, a path can be made,
One step at a time, with intuition's aid.

The Unspoken Dream

The dream lies dormant, a whisper untold,
A yearning for something, braver than bold.
Fear holds it captive, in a cage built so tight,
Leaving potential hidden, from the morning's light.
The weight of the world, a burden of doubt,
Stifles the whispers, leaving dreams without clout.
Hope's fragile seed, planted deep in the soul,
Struggles to blossom, yearning to make itself whole.
But wait, in the silence, a strength takes its stand,
A voice urging courage, to break free from the sand.
The unspoken dream, awakens with might,
Ready to bloom, bathed in the sun's golden light.

The Faded Song

The melody lingers, a whisper of sound,
A song once so vibrant, now lost and unbound.
Notes scattered and forgotten, a rhythm astray,
A forgotten passion, lost in the day.
The weight of the world, a burden of time,
Steals the music's magic, leaving a rhyme.
Hope's fragile voice, strained and unheard,
Yearning for an audience, a comforting word.
But wait, in the silence, a rhythm takes hold,
A spark of inspiration, a story untold.
The faded song echoes, a memory's embrace,
A chance to revive it, with a newfound grace.

Whispers in the Static (a different take)

The static crackles and hisses, a chaotic embrace,
Drowning out voices, with an unsettling pace.
Signals distorted, a message unclear,
Leaving the listener stranded, with doubt and with fear.
The weight of the world, a burden of noise,
Distracts from the whispers, from the heart's gentle voice.
Hope's fragile signal, lost in the fray,
Yearning for connection, to find its own way.
But wait, in the static, a rhythm breaks through,
A message of patience, urging one to pursue.
For even in chaos, a voice can be heard,
A chance for connection, a comforting word.

The Weathered Book

The pages are worn, the spine cracked and frayed,
A story etched deeply, a wisdom displayed.
Ink-stained memories, whispered in lines,
Of battles fought bravely, and love that entwines.
The weight of the world, a burden of years,
Fills every chapter, with laughter and tears.
Hope's fragile thread, woven through the tale,
A testament to resilience, that won't ever fail.
But wait, in the turning, a message unfolds,
A whisper of courage, in stories untold.
For even the weathered, hold wisdom within,
A legacy cherished, where strength can begin.

Whispers in the Snow

The snowflakes descend, a silent ballet,
A world wrapped in white, on this winter's display.
Each flake a soft whisper, a story untold,
Of beauty found softly, in the season's cold.
The weight of the world, a burden of white,
Seems to hush anxieties, fading from sight.
Hope's fragile snowflake, lands soft on the ground,
A promise of new beginnings, when spring can be found.
But wait, in the stillness, a warmth takes its hold,
A reminder of resilience, braver than bold.
For even in frozen landscapes, life finds a way,
Seeds slumbering dreams, waiting for a brighter day.

The Untamed Flame

The fire roars fiercely, a wild, untamed beast,
Crackling and popping, a passionate feast.
Warmth radiates outward, defying the night,
A symbol of strength, bathed in the golden light.
The weight of the world, a burden of chill,
Seeks solace in flames, dispelling the ill.
Hope's fragile spark, ignites into view,
A beacon of defiance, chasing the blue.
But wait, in the crackling, a message ignites,
A call for control, where passion takes flight.
For even the untamed, can be harnessed with care,
Guiding its power, a future to share.

The Faded Tapestry

The threads hang loose, a tapestry worn,
Colors once vibrant, now weathered and torn.
Images blurred, a story unclear,
A reminder of moments, both precious and dear.
The weight of the world, a burden of time,
Frays the edges of memory, leaving a rhyme.
Hope's fragile thread, a whisper of hue,
Yearning to mend the tapestry, make it brand new.
But wait, in the remnants, a beauty remains,
A symphony woven, of laughter and pains.
For even the faded, holds stories untold,
A reminder of journeys, braver than bold.

Whispers in the Dawn

The first light awakens, chasing away night,
A canvas of orange, replacing the fright.
Birdsong fills the air, a melody sweet,
A whisper of hope, a brand new world to greet.
The weight of the world, seems lighter somehow,
As darkness surrenders, to the sun's gentle vow.
Hope's fragile wings, unfurl and take flight,
Ready to soar upwards, bathed in the morning's light.
But wait, in the rising, a message takes hold,
A reminder of cycles, a story untold.
For even the darkest night, yields to the dawn,
And with each new sunrise, a chance to be reborn.

In Conclusion

Life's tapestry is woven with threads of joy and sorrow, triumph and despair. Through these poems, we've explored the spectrum of human experience, traversing the depths of hardship and the heights of hope. We've witnessed the resilience of the human spirit, its ability to weather storms and emerge stronger, forever marked yet unbroken.

"Wounds of Life" is not a chronicle of despair, but a testament to the enduring human spirit. It is a celebration of our capacity to heal, to find hope in the midst of darkness, and to emerge transformed by our struggles. For even the deepest wounds can become sources of strength, shaping us into the courageous and compassionate beings we are meant to be.

As you close this book, remember that the whispers of hope and resilience echo within you. Carry them with you as you navigate your own life's journey, and know that you are braver than you believe, stronger than you seem, and loved more than you know. May these poems serve as a reminder that you are not alone in your struggles, and that within you lies the power to heal and create a life filled with beauty and meaning.

About the Author

Mrigendra Bharti, born on June 29, 2004, in South Delhi, India, is a multifaceted individual recognized as the owner of Mrigendra Bharti Group InfoTech India Co. Pvt Ltd. Beyond his entrepreneurial endeavors, he is a distinguished music producer, director, and a budding writer.

Embarking on his professional journey at a young age, Mrigendra Bharti's visionary leadership has led to the establishment of several successful ventures, including Croma Music Series Entertainment, Sellbrochure, Fauget Innovative, and more.

What sets Mrigendra apart is his early initiation into the world of business. His foray into the unknown realms of entrepreneurship began during his 10th-grade years, where he delved into the music industry. This initial venture laid the foundation for subsequent achievements, showcasing his dedication and resilience.

Having honed his skills in music, Mrigendra Bharti not only demonstrated significant growth in his craft but also expanded his professional network. His passion extends beyond music, encompassing app and website development, as well as graphic design.

Fueled by his creative aspirations, Mrigendra established the Mrigendra Bharti Group, a company specializing in website and app development. Currently, he collaborates with a dedicated team, collectively working on ambitious projects that promise innovation and excellence.

Mrigendra's journey serves as an inspiration, particularly for today's students, highlighting the potential of youthful determination and the ability to transform innovative ideas into successful businesses. As he continues to make strides in various domains, Mrigendra Bharti remains a dynamic force, contributing vibrancy to the realms of business, music, and technology.

Read more at https://www.imwriter-mrigendra.rf.gd.